HIGGINS • PRASETYA • SILAS • HERMS
ORLANDO • HOWELL • LAWSON • VALENZA

VOLUME TWO

SPECIAL THANKS TO
BRIAN CASENTINI, MELISSA FLORES, EDGAR PASTEN, PAUL STRICKLAND, MARCY GEORGE, JASON BISCHOFF AND EVERYONE AT **SABAN BRANDS**.

BOOM! STUDIOS   SABAN Brands

MIGHTY MORPHIN POWER RANGERS Volume Two, March 2017. Published by BOOM! Studios, a division of Boom Entertainment, Inc.

A catalog record of this book is available from OCLC and from the BOOM! Studios website, www.boom-studios.com, on the Librarians Page.

BOOM! Studios, 5670 Wilshire Boulevard, Suite 450, Los Angeles, CA 90036-5679. Printed in China. First Printing. ISBN: 978-1-60886-942-8, eISBN: 978-1-61398-613-4

WRITTEN BY
KYLE HIGGINS

ILLUSTRATED BY
THONY SILAS CHAPTER 5
HENDRY PRASETYA CHAPTERS 6-8

COLORS BY
BRYAN VALENZA CHAPTER 5
MATT HERMS CHAPTERS 6-8

LETTERS BY
ED DUKESHIRE

COVER BY
GOÑI MONTES

DESIGNER
JILLIAN CRAB

ASSISTANT EDITOR
MATTHEW LEVINE

ASSOCIATE EDITOR
ALEX GALER

EDITOR
DAFNA PLEBAN

NE MONTH BEFORE TOMMY IVER CAME TO ANGEL GROVE...
<--BUT THAT SHOULD NOT DETER US! FOR TOO LONG, WE AS A SOCIETY HAVE GIVEN IN TO FEAR!>*
<AND I HAVE WATCHED AS THIS FEAR OF MOON WITCHES AND MONSTERS HAS AFFECTED US! WELL, I SAY NO MORE! THE ITALIAN PEOPLE WILL NOT BOW DOWN TO RITA REPULSA!>
PRESIDENZA DE
* TRANSLATED FROM ITALIAN.
<SHE CANNOT BREAK OUR WILL! SHE CANNOT BREAK OUR SPIRIT!>
<THERE IS NOTHING SHE CAN DO TO MAKE US AFRAID OF HER!>

A SHORT TIME LATER...
‹I LOVE THOSE WHO CAN SMILE IN TROUBLE!›

<NOTHING STRENGTHENS AUTHORITY SO MUCH AS SILENCE!>
<I-I THINK IT'S SUPPOSED TO BE THE VITRUVIAN MAN?!>
<SIR! WE HAVE TO EVACUATE RIGHT NOW-->
<THE NOBLEST PLEASURE IS THE JOY OF UNDER-STANDING-->
GHHH!

TRINI, GET THE HAND GYROS READY! WE'RE GONNA NEED--
JASON, ON YOUR *THREE!* HE'S COMING *BACK*--
<THE KNOWLEDGE OF ALL THINGS *IS* POSSIBLE!>
<BUT THE GREATEST DECEPTION MEN SUFFER IS FROM THEIR OWN OPINIONS!>

<BLINDING IGNORANCE DOES MISLEAD US! WRETCHED MORTALS, OPEN YOUR EYES!>
OKAY, MY ITALIAN'S PRETTY RUSTY--
--BUT IS THIS GUY JUST, LIKE, RECITING DA VINCI QUOTES?
IT DOESN'T MATTER!
"HE'S GOT A CLEAR LINE AT THE PRIME MINISTER!"
<AS ALWAYS, IT IS *EASIER* TO RESIST AT THE BEGINNING-->
<--THAN IT IS AT THE *END*!>
AHHHH!

<MY SOUL ACHES!>
COME ON! WE'RE GOING TO TELEPORT OUT OF HERE!
NO! NOT WITHOUT MY PEOPLE!
<OUR LIFE IS MADE-->
<--BY THE DEATH OF OTHERS!>

YEAH, ZACK!
<I THOUGHT...I WAS LEARNING TO LIVE...BUT I...WAS ONLY LEARNING TO DIE...>
I MEAN THIS IN THE BEST POSSIBLE WAY-- LITERALLY A KILLER SWIPE.
HEH. THANKS...
GRACI! GRACI, RED RANGER!
CI SALVATO, RED RANGER!
GO GO, RED RANGER!

HM.
MY EMPRESS.
THE VITRUVIAN SHOULD HAVE BEEN ARMORED, AND HIS LANGUAGE NOT ENTRUSTED TO WHAT BABOO AND SQUATT FOUND ON THE INTERNET. I'VE ALREADY SPOKEN TO FINSTER--HE HAS A FOLLOW-UP IN THE WORKS, AND CAN BE READY--
NO.
I THINK I HAVE A BETTER IDEA.

WHAT THE--
ALL RIGHT, LET'S DO--
WHAK
UHNN!
TAKE HIM.

UHNNN...
AW, MAN...
I'M SORRY ABOUT THE AMBUSH, ZACK. BUT YOU HAVE MY WORD...
...I COME IN PEACE.
SOMEHOW I *DOUBT* THAT.
NO, NO. NO TRICKS. IF YOU CHECK, YOU'LL SEE YOU STILL HAVE YOUR POWER COIN.
YOU CAN LEAVE AT ANY TIME. OF COURSE, IF YOU'RE AT ***ALL*** INTERESTED IN WHAT I HAVE TO SAY THOUGH...
WHAT IS THIS?

LIKE I SAID--I JUST WANT TO TALK.
I WAS IMPRESSED BY HOW YOU HANDLED THINGS IN ITALY, ZACK. AND I WANTED TO CONGRATULATE YOU. PERSONALLY. AFTER ALL--
--YOU'RE THE REAL REASON THE RANGERS WON TODAY.
IT WAS A TEAM EFFORT.
SURE. BUT YOU WERE THE ONE PILOTING THE MEGAZORD WHEN JASON DECIDED TO RUN OFF TO BE A GLORY HOUND.
WITHOUT YOU, MY DA VINCI MONSTER STOMPS ON HIM AND THE PRIME MINISTER. RIGHT?
YOU KNOW, I THINK WE MAY HAVE GOTTEN OFF ON THE WRONG FOOT. WHY DON'T YOU LET ME SHOW YOU SOMETHING?
UNLESS, OF COURSE, YOU DON'T THINK YOU CAN HANDLE IT.

THIS IS--
MY PALACE. WELL, PART OF IT, ANYWAY.
WHEN YOU'RE TRAPPED IN A DUMPSTER FOR TEN THOUSAND YEARS, YOU COME TO APPRECIATE OPEN FLOOR PLANS.
AM I SUPPOSED TO FEEL SORRY FOR YOU?
IT'S MINE! LEGGO!
LOOK, I DON'T WANT ALL THI DESTRUCTION AND BAD BLOO BETWEEN US. BUT...ZORDON HASN'T GIVEN M MUCH CHOICE
AWW...
THAT'S KIND OF HIS THING. HE DOESN'T REALLY GIVE PEOPLE CHOICES.
YOU'RE THE ONES WHO STARTED ATTACKING OUR WORLD WITH GIANT MONSTERS. WHAT CHOICE WAS THERE?
MY EMPRESS DIDN'T START MAKING THEM BIG UNTIL ZORDON GOT ZORDS. YOU DON'T KNOW THE WHOLE STORY.
THAT'S A LIE.

LISTEN, ALL I'M TRYING TO SAY IS THAT I BELIEVE PEOPLE NEED TO REACH THEIR TRUE POTENTIAL. UNDER *MY* LEADERSHIP, THAT CAN HAPPEN. EARTH CAN THRIVE.
YEAH, I'M NOT SURE "THRIVE" MEANS WHAT YOU *THINK* IT MEANS.
JUST LOOK AT YOUR WORLD AS IT EXISTS *NOW.* IS IT *REALLY* THAT GREAT OF A PLACE?
AND THAT'S TO SAY NOTHING OF THE AFTERMATH OF *OUR* SKIRMISHES.
BUT WE CAN MAKE IT STOP. *WE* CAN SOLVE THIS WORLD'S PROBLEMS, ZACK.
"WE?"
I THINK YOU CAN BE *MORE,* ZACK. YOU *SHOULD* BE MORE.
AND ON *MY* TEAM...

...YOU CAN BE.
I KNOW WHAT IT'S LIKE TO BE A SECOND IN COMMAND, WHO HAS WHAT IT TAKES TO LEAD. YOU AND I ARE KINDRED SPIRITS.
AND MAKE NO MISTAKE--THAT'S WHAT I'M OFFERING HERE. A CHANCE TO LEAD US...
...TO A BETTER WORLD.

THERE'S A PLACE FOR RANGERS HELPING THE PEOPLE OF EARTH, ZACK. I'VE NEVER BELIEVED OTHERWISE. BUT IT SHOULD BE THE *RIGHT* RANGER, WITH THE RIGHT *GUIDANCE.*
AND THE CATCH TO ALL THIS?
NO CATCH. WELL, EXCEPT THAT MY DRAGON COIN BRINGS WITH IT *UNBELIEVABLE* POWER. AND IN ORDER TO FUEL YOU *WITH* IT...
...YOU'D HAVE TO FIRST PART WITH *YOUR* POWERS. *WILLINGLY.*
SO YOU WANT ME TO TURN AGAINST ZORDON. AND MY *FRIENDS.*
ONCE WE SECURE THE WORLD, THEY'LL SEE THAT YOU DID THIS TO HELP THEM. THEY'LL UNDERSTAND, ZACK.
THAT YOU DID IT FOR THE GOOD OF *EVERYONE.*
YOU'RE RIGHT.
WE *SHOULD* BE DOING MORE.
VERY SMART, ZACK. YOU'RE MAKING THE RIGHT CHOICE...
I KNOW.

YOU UNGRATEFUL BRAT!
GAHHH!
YOU HAVE NO IDEA WHAT YOU'RE TURNING DOWN!
YEAH... HUFF HUFF I'M GOOD.
UHH!
DESTROY HIM!
KRAKK

HAVE YOU ALERTED THE OTHERS?
NO. I... WANTED TO TALK TO YOU GUYS FIRST, BEFORE I TELL THEM ANYTHING. I MEAN, IF RITA REALLY CAN CREATE A NEW RANGER...
YES. THE CONSEQUENCES WOULD BE DRASTIC.
SO... WE SHOULD TELL THEM, RIGHT?
YES. BUT I'D ASK THAT YOU ALLOW ME TIME TO ASSESS THE SITUATION AND RITA'S CAPABILITIES, BEFORE WE ALARM ANYONE.
AYE-YI-YI. OH, ZACK. I'M SO SORRY.
THE WHOLE EXPERIENCE SOUNDS JUST TERRIBLE!
YEAH...
THE WEIRDEST PART IS THOUGH, IF I'M BEING TOTALLY HONEST...THE THINGS SHE SHOWED ME... WHAT SHE PROMISED...
PART OF ME WAS TEMPTED. AND I DON'T KNOW WHAT THAT MEANS.
IT MEANS YOU ARE HUMAN, ZACK. YOU HOPE AND WISH THE BEST FOR THE WORLD. THAT IS UNDENIABLE, AND AN ADMIRABLE QUALITY.
IT'S WHY I AM HONORED TO WORK WITH YOU AS A POWER RANGER.
THANKS...

I CAN SENSE THERE IS SOMETHING ELSE WEIGHING ON YOU THOUGH.
I NEED TO DO MORE, ZORDON.
I DON'T CARE ABOUT LEADING. IT'S NOT LIKE THAT.
I JUST MEAN...WE HAVE ALL THIS GREAT POWER...I WANT TO DO MORE FOR THE WORLD.
I UNDERSTAND, ZACK. THEN ALLOW ME TO CONSIDER HOW. ALL OF OUR ACTIONS CARRY CONSEQUENCES AND REPERCUSSIONS.
THERE IS NO TELLING...

"...WHAT UNINTENDED EFFECTS THEY COULD HAVE."
HEYYY! LOOK WHO FINALLY DECIDED TO JOIN!
YOUR EARS MUST HAVE BEEN RINGING. WE WERE JUST TALKING ABOUT YOU.
...O-OH YEAH?
YEAH, MAN. SIT DOWN AND ORDER SOMETHING. I'M BUYING. LEAST I CAN DO FOR THE WAY YOU BAILED ME OUT TODAY.
WITHOUT YOU, ME AND THE PRIME MINISTER ARE FOOTPRINTS.
OH. I'M...SURE YOU WOULD HAVE FIGURED SOMETHING OUT...
I DON'T KNOW. HE LOOKED PRETTY FOOTPRINT-READY TO ME...
FOR REAL, MAN. THE RANGERS AREN'T THE RANGERS WITHOUT YOU.
...THAT'S... PRETTY COOL OF YOU TO SAY. THANKS.
HEY, IT'S THE TRUTH. NOW HURRY UP AND ORDER SOMETHING.
PREFERABLY NOT ITALIAN.
HA.
"IT'S SETTLED THEN..."

...WE'LL NEED A BLANK SLATE. SOMEONE WHO ISN'T ALREADY A POWER RANGER. AN OUTSIDER. SOMEONE...
...NEW...
HE'LL LEAVE YOU.
WHAT--?
HE'LL TURN HIS BACK. HE'LL JOIN THEM.
WHO ARE YOU? WHO DARES SPEAK TO ME LIKE THIS?! SHOW YOURSELF!
WHEN YOU'RE TRULY READY TO RULE EARTH...WHEN YOU REALIZE I'M RIGHT...
...THEN YOU WILL SEE ME.

AN FRANCISCO.
HE AFTERMATH.
--WITH MEDICAL AND EMERGENCY RESPONDERS ALREADY AT WORK.
IF YOU'RE AN EAST BAY RESIDENT, CITY OFFICIALS ARE URGING YOU TO STAY HOME.
WHY'D WE HAVE TO MOVE TO ANGEL GROVE...
TOMMY! I DON'T HEAR THAT SHOWER RUNNING!

YOU BETTER NOT STILL BE IN BED.
KNOCK KNOCK
STAFF ONLY
KEEP OUT
TOMMY, I SWEAR IF YOU'RE NOT UP IN FIVE--
STAFF ONLY
KEEP OUT
"I AM THE BLACK DRAGON."

I WOULD OFFER YOU ONE CHANCE TO SURRENDER.
BUT I THINK WE KNOW WHAT YOUR ANSWER WOULD BE.

I DON'T KNOW WHAT YOU ARE, OR WHERE YOU'RE FROM, BUT YOU JUST WRECKED OUR HOME.
THERE'S NOT A CHANCE IN HELL WE'RE SURRENDERING.
THEN IT'S SETTLED. GOOD.
I'D THINK LESS OF YOU OTHERWISE.

AHHHHH!
YAIII!
K-KIM... GHH C-CAN YOU--
--HNN Y-YEAH!

KOOM
GO! GO! GO!
KOOM
KOOM
KOOM

UHNN!
ARH!
KOOM
TOMMY, WATCH--
UHN!
WHAP

GHN!
ARRRR!
SHUNK
AHH!
WHAM

LAST... CHANCE...
PASS.
GHN!
CRRKK
UHN!
JASON... WE NEED TO R-RETREAT...

"...BEFORE THIS GETS ANY WORSE."
THE GREEN RANGER. ALWAYS SO DIFFERENT.
UNIQUE.
HRK!
I CAN GET US TO THE POCKET DIMENSION-- TELEPORTATION'S STILL ONLINE.
ROUTE ALL NECESSARY SYSTEMS THERE. THE COMMAND CENTER'S EXPOSED.
"WE GOTTA MAKE SURE HE CAN'T FOLLOW US."
LET'S MAKE YOU A BIT MORE NORMAL.
GYAAAHHH!!

WHAKK
LET GO!
EVERYBODY HOLD ON! I'M GETTING US OUTTA HERE!
NOT SO FAST.
WHA--
NO!

I ONLY NEED ONE OF YOU.
YOU'LL DO FINE, BILLY.
YAII!
WE'RE READY FOR YOU, EMPRESS.

WHOA, WHAT HAPPENED TO THIS PLACE?
WITHOUT ZORDON, EVERYTHING HE BUILT THE LAST TIME WE WERE HERE...
...IS FALLING APART.
THAT WAS... I DON'T EVEN KNOW HOW TO DESCRIBE WHAT JUST HAPPENED.
IT WAS LIKE, SOMEONE WAS PEELING MY SKIN OFF WITH A KNIFE. I'VE NEVER...I DIDN'T KNOW OUR POWERS COULD BE SEPARATED LIKE THAT.
ARE YOU OKAY?
YEAH. JUST... RATTLED...
WHERE'S BILLY?

HE WAS HELPING KIM, RIGHT BEFORE WE STARTED TELEPORTING--
DID HE MAKE IT CLEAR?
I-I *THOUGHT* SO--
DID YOU SEE *HIM* TELEPORT?
I DON'T KNOW! I THOUGHT HE DID!
JASON, WE GOTTA GO BACK! BEFORE--
THEY'RE... ALREADY *THERE*...

GREAT. THIS IS JUST...
WE...LOST ZORDON AND ALPHA, THERE'S SOME DRAGON WHO CAN TURN US INSIDE OUT, AND NOW HE'S GOT THE COMMAND CENTER AND THE ONE GUY WHO MIGHT BE ABLE TO FIGURE OUT WHAT'S GOING ON...
IN ALL THE STUFF YOU'VE SEEN FROM RITA--THE TIME YOU WERE WITH HER, THE HALLUCINATIONS, ALL OF IT--IS THERE ANYTHING THAT MIGHT TELL US WHAT SHE'S PLANNING? OR WHAT THIS BLACK DRAGON ACTUALLY IS?
SCORPINA SAID...THE CRYSTAL CHARGED ON GREEN CHAOS ENERGY.
AND THAT'S WHAT OPENED THE PORTAL.
YEAH.
SO THIS DRAGON THING IS TIED TO YOU. SOMEHOW.
SOMEHOW.
POWER RANGERS
BUT YOU HAVE NO IDEA HOW.
NO, ZACK. I DON'T.

OH MY GOD IF YOU GUYS DON'T CHILL OUT SOMEBODY'S GONNA SLIP ON THE TESTOSTERONE AND BREAK THEIR NECK.
WE'RE SUPPOSED TO BE *FRIENDS.* AND RIGHT NOW, ONE OF OUR FRIENDS IS IN *TROUBLE.*
SO RATHER THAN EVERYBODY THROWING *SHADE,* WHY DON'T WE FOCUS ON HOW WE'RE GOING TO *SAVE* HIM?
YEAH...
YEAH... SORRY... YOU'RE RIGHT...
BILLY... ALPHA...ZORDON... WE'VE NEVER HAD TO...I MEAN...THIS IS AS BAD AS ANYTHING RITA'S PULLED OFF BEFORE.
I KNOW.
HOW *ARE* WE GOING TO GET THEM BACK?

RUINING THE COMMAND CENTER. DESTROYING ZORDON. CHASING THE RANGERS *OUT.*
I'LL ADMIT, WHEN YOU FIRST CONTACTED ME...I WAS SKEPTICAL OF WHAT YOU OFFERED. BUT WITH THE EXCEPTION OF LOSING SCORPINA, THIS HAS GONE EVEN BETTER THAN I ***EXPECTED.***
EMPRESS. *WELCOME.*
THE REMAINING RANGERS HAVE FLED TO A POCKET DIMENSION. AND REROUTED THEIR CONTROL SYSTEMS THERE.
SO WE CANNOT FOLLOW THEM.
NO. BUT WE DON'T NEED TO.
POWER RANGERS

WHAT ARE YOU DOING?
USING THE BLUE RANGER'S POWER COIN AS AN ACCESS POINT.
TO THE MORPHIN GRID.

WE'VE GOT NO IDEA WHAT KIND OF SHAPE ALPHA'S IN. OR ZORDON. IF HE...EVEN SURVIVED.
BILLY'S THE PRIORITY.
BUT THERE'S NO SIGN OF HIM AT THE COMMAND CENTER?
NO. SO, IF I HAD TO GUESS...
THE DARK DIMENSION.
YEAH. THEY'RE PROBABLY HOLDING HIM IN THERE. WHICH MEANS WE NEED TO FIGURE OUT A WAY TO GET IN BEFORE--
AHHHHHHH!
W-WHAT JUST HAPPENED...

...TO YOUR POWERS...?

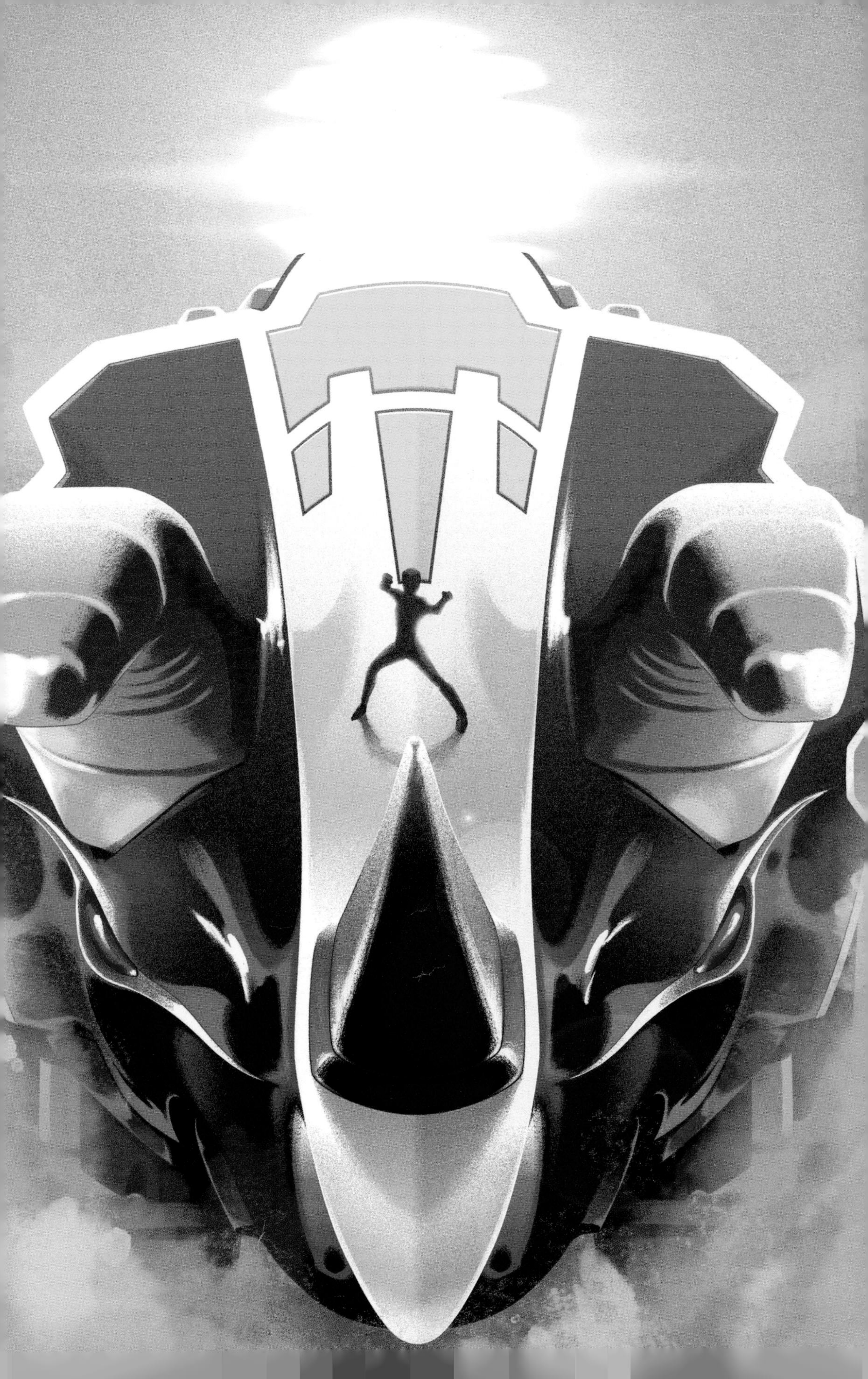

SCRAPE
H-HELLO?
I-IS SOMEONE ELSE IN HERE?

WORRY. GIVE IT ENOUGH TIME...
...AND YOU'LL FEEL RIGHT AT HOME.
ARE YOU... CHAINED UP?
I FAILED MY QUEEN AND LOST HER GREEN RANGER. I WELCOME MY SHACKLES. HER PUNISHMENT IS JUST.
BUT...YOU'VE FAILED RITA BEFORE. A LOT. WHY IS THIS DIFFERENT?
...
WORRY ABOUT YOURSELF, BLUE RANGER.
BEFORE YOU LOSE YOUR MOUTH AS WELL.

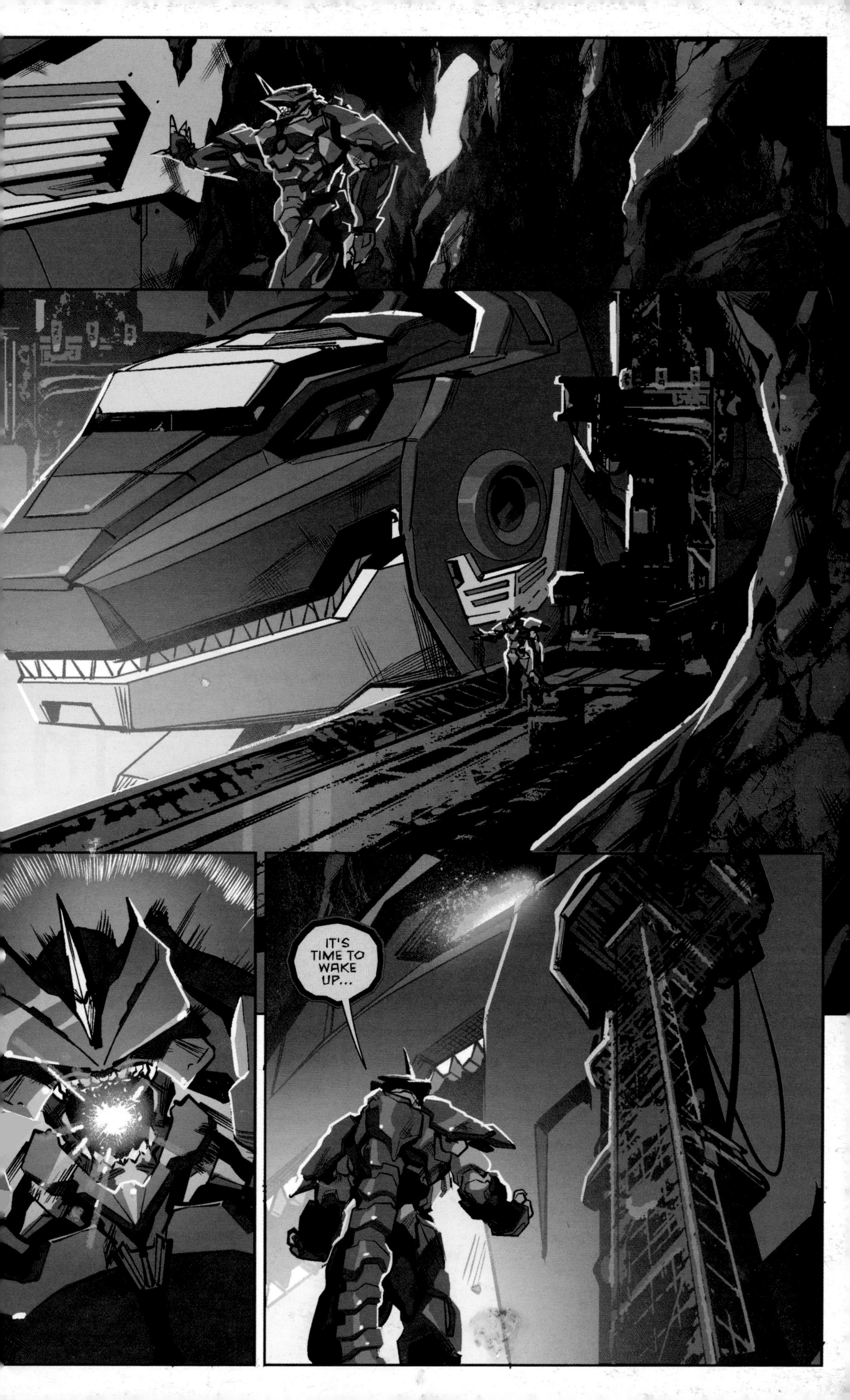
IT'S TIME TO WAKE UP...

ONE ON TOP OF THE OTHER! YES! YES! JUST LIKE THAT!
FWOOOOM
FWOOOM
VERY GOOD, BOYS! WELL DONE!
WHO'S NEXT?! HURRY NOW! EMPRESS RITA WANTS THIS WALL UP YESTERDAY!
WE ALL MUST MAKE SACRIFICES!
CENTERED! CENTERED! IT NEEDS TO BE DIRECTLY WHERE THAT OLD FOOL'S TUBE WAS!
YES... PERFECT.

AHHHH. IT'S GOOD TO BE THE QUEEN.
WOULDN'T YOU AGREE?
OF COURSE, YOU DIDN'T HAVE THE FIRST CLUE WHAT YOU WERE MISSING OUT ON. BLINDLY SERVING THE OLD SAGE LONG AFTER HE KNEW WHAT WAS GOOD FOR ANYONE. LOOK HOW WRONG YOU WERE.
WHEN YOU'RE FINISHED MELTING THE ROBOT DOWN, USE HIS ALLOYS TO FASHION A LAMP.
AT LEAST THEN HE'LL BE USEFUL FOR ONCE IN HIS EXISTENCE.

ANYTHING?

NO. I...DON'T THINK THE PROBLEM'S WITH THE MORPHERS, EITHER.
BUT OUR POWER SCANS--

ARE ALL FINE. I KNOW. BUT THE MORPHERS ALSO SEEM FINE.
I THINK.

I'M DOING THE BEST I CAN, BUT THIS...ZORDON, OR ALPHA, OR BILLY COULD FIGURE THIS OUT, BUT...
IT'S OKAY. WE'LL CRACK THIS. SOMEHOW. AND THEN WE'LL GET BILLY BACK AND GO FROM THERE.

ALL RIGHT. WELL...I THINK THE PROBLEM IS WITH HOW WE CONNECT TO THE MORPHIN GRID. SOMEHOW...WE'VE BEEN CUT OFF FROM IT.
YOU CAN TELL THAT?
WELL...NO. BUT TOMMY'S POWERS ARE TIED TO THE GRID IN A DIFFERENT WAY THAN OURS.

"AND HE'S THE ONLY ONE THAT STILL HAS THEM."
HELMETS BACK ON! BEFORE--
I DON'T SEE HOW WATCHING THAT IS HEALTHY.
I TOOK DOWN SCORPINA, BROKE THE DRAGON DAGGER, AND TOOK AWAY HER CRYSTAL...HER CRYSTAL THAT SHE TOLD ME WAS POWERED BY GREEN CHAOS ENERGY.
SO, THEN WHAT DO I DO?
TOMMY...
I GOT MAD AT ZACK AND JASON AND GO OFF THE DEEP END. AND NOW...
...YEAH.

SO MUCH FOR MAKING A KILLER FIRST IMPRESSION, HUH?
ACTUALLY, TECHNICALLY, YOUR FIRST IMPRESSION *DID* INVOLVE TRYING TO KILL US...
I JUST...I JUST WANTED TO DO A GOOD JOB. YOU KNOW THAT, RIGHT?
YEAH. I KNOW. I THINK *EVERYONE* KNOWS. EVEN IF THEY CAN'T ADMIT IT. WE'RE ALL JUST...GETTING USED TO THINGS STILL.
WE WERE A PRETTY GOOD TEAM BEFORE. SOMETIMES IT TAKES *TIME* FOR PEOPLE TO COME AROUND ON NEW THINGS.
RIGHT NOW YOU'RE LITERALLY THE *ONLY* ONE OF US THAT STILL HAS POWERS, TOMMY. SOMETHING TELLS ME YOU'LL HAVE ANOTHER CHANCE TO *PROVE* YOURSELF.
HELLO, PEOPLE OF *EARTH.*

I COME TO YOU LIVE, IN WHATEVER LANGUAGE IS NATIVE TO YOUR AREA.
AHH THE JOYS OF INTERGALACTIC TECHNOLOGY. BRINGING CREATURES FROM ALL WALKS OF LIFE, TOGETHER.
THE MESSAGE I HAVE FOR YOU TODAY IS TRULY ONE OF UNITY.
FOR TOO LONG, THIS WAR OF OURS HAS GONE ON.
WHICH IS WHY I'M GIVING YOUR WORLD LEADERS TWENTY-FOUR HOURS TO STAND DOWN AND PLEDGE ALLEGIANCE TO ME. BEFORE I DESTROY THEM ALL.
NOW, FOR THOSE OF YOU ASKING THE OBVIOUS QUESTION...NO, THE POWER RANGERS WILL NOT COME TO YOUR RESCUE.
THE RANGERS ARE GONE. DESTROYED. AND IN THEIR PLACE...
...I HAVE TAKEN OVER THEIR HOME.
OH, AND THEIR ZORDS...

RAAAAR
...ARE ALSO MINE.
RWWARR
109
カラオケ
SO, TO THE PRESIDENTS, THE KINGS, THE DICTATORS. STARTING RIGHT NOW, YOU HAVE TWENTY-FOUR HOURS TO COME TO YOUR SENSES. ANY NATION THAT DOES NOT PLEDGE LOYALTY, WILL BECOME MY ENEMY.
AND I *WILL* CONQUER YOU BY *FORCE*. ONE WAY OR ANOTHER...
...YOUR PEOPLE *WILL* SERVE *THE QUEEN*.

WHETHER OR NOT YOU'RE ALIVE TO JOIN THEM IS UP TO YOU.
GUYS, ARE YOU SEEING--
YEAH... WE SAW THE WHOLE THING.
SHE'S GOT THE ZORDS NOW, TOO! HOW IS SHE DOING THIS?!
IT'S THAT BLACK DRAGON THING--IT HAS TO BE.
ARE YOU GUYS ANY CLOSER ON THE POWERS FRONT?
TRINI THINKS THERE'S SOMETHING INTERFERING WITH HOW WE ACCESS THE MORPHIN GRID. WHICH IS WHY YOUR POWERS AREN'T AFFECTED.
BUT I DON'T KNOW THE FIRST PLACE TO START.
BILLY'S THE ONLY ONE THAT WOULD EVEN HAVE A CLUE, AND I CAN'T EVEN PINPOINT WHERE HE IS.
IF HE'S ALIVE... SHE'LL HAVE HIM IN THE DARK DIMENSION. YOU'VE GOTTA LET ME GO AFTER HIM, JASON.
...CAN YOU ACTUALLY GET INSIDE THE DARK DIMENSION?
WELL...THERE'S A PORTAL GENERATOR IN RITA'S MOON BASE. AND WITH RITA TAKING OVER AND FORTIFYING THE COMMAND CENTER, I'D BET SERIOUS MONEY ON THE MOON BASE BEING LIGHT ON STAFF.
BUT YOU CAN'T JUST, LIKE, TELEPORT IN. AND LET'S NOT FORGET, THE PLACE IS CALLED THE MOON BASE FOR A REASON.
HOW THE HECK ARE YOU GOING TO GET TO IT?

SCRAWRRR

YOU KNOW, I ALWAYS KNEW THE ZORDS WERE SPACE CAPABLE IN *THEORY,* BUT...
PILOTING ONE UP HERE IS A WHOLE OTHER THING.
FOR *SURE.*

KEEP THE ENGINE RUNNING!
GOOD LUCK!

Palace
WELCOME BACK, TOMMY.

DO YOU THINK... ZORDON'S STILL ALIVE SOMEWHERE?
I DON'T KNOW. I MEAN, WE'VE BEEN CUT OFF FROM HIM BEFORE, AND ENERGY CAN'T, YOU KNOW, ACTUALLY BE DESTROYED...
BUT I DON'T ACTUALLY HAVE THE FIRST CLUE WHAT I'M EVEN LOOKING FOR. IF BILLY WAS HERE...
YOU'RE DOING FINE, TRINI. JUST...TAKE A SECOND. RELAX. YOU'VE BEEN RUNNING YOURSELF RAGGED.
I SHOULDN'T HAVE TALKED JASON INTO RETREATING. WE SHOULD HAVE STAYED AND FOUGHT AT THE COMMAND CENTER. CALLED OUR ZORDS AND--
--POSSIBLY GOTTEN OURSELVES WIPED OUT. WE DON'T KNOW WHAT THIS BLACK DRAGON THING IS YET, BUT HE HAD OUR NUMBER. WE HAD TO RETREAT.
LOOK, I KNOW IT'S EASY TO THINK YOU SHOULD HAVE HANDLED STUFF DIFFERENTLY. TRUST ME.
BUT NOW... IT'S ABOUT HOW WE ADAPT. WE JUST GOTTA KEEP GRINDING AND EVENTUALLY SOMETHING WILL BREAK OUR WAY. IT HAS TO--
...WHAT THE...
IS THAT...
BDEET BDEET
...ALPHA?!

ROCKET FINGERS. OH YEAH.
AH, JASON I'M GUESSING. FACING ME WITHOUT POWERS. WELL...

...IF YOU INSIST.

NO!
JASON!
LET HIM GO, TOMMY. RIGHT NOW...
UHN!

...YOU HAVE A MUCH *BIGGER* PROBLEM ON YOUR HANDS.

CHAPTER **EIGHT**

JAMAL CAMPBELL | ISSUE EIGHT COVER

--FOR THOSE OF YOU TUNING IN, HOPING FOR AN EXCLUSIVE NEW VIDEO OF THE RANGERS, ONE THAT *DISPROVES* RITA'S CLAIMS OF THEIR DEFEAT...
YOU'RE OUT OF LUCK.
THESE ARE DARK TIMES, RANGER STATION FOLLOWERS. DARK TIMES INDEED.
YOU SAID IT, SKULL.
"WITH RITA'S TWENTY-FOUR HOUR DEADLINE LOOMING, WORLD LEADERS ARE *SCRAMBLING.*
"SEVERAL MILITARY CAMPAIGNS HAVE ALREADY BEEN ATTEMPTED, INCLUDING *THIS* ONE IN TOKYO."

"AND WHAT ABOUT US, HERE IN THE RANGER CAPITAL?
SINCE THE ASSAULT IN THE BAY, THERE'S BEEN NO SIGN OF THE GREEN RANGER *OR* HIS DRAGONZORD.
SO JUST WHAT ***HAPPENED?*** HOW DID RITA REGAIN CONTROL OF THE DRAGONZORD? AND WHERE IS IT NOW?

"...IS HE STILL OUT THERE SOMEWHERE?"
YOU HAD IT ALL, TOMMY.
UHHNN!

THE EMPRESS GAVE YOU EVERYTHING, AND YOU TURNED YOUR BACK ON HER.
AND FOR WHAT? TO DIE HERE, ALONE, ON THE MOON--
YEAH, THAT'S DEFINITELY NOT PART OF THE PLAN!
DRAGON-SHIELD--DISENGAG
JASON! WHAT'S YOUR STATUS?!
WORKING EHNN ON IT! TRYING TO GET THE DRAGONZORD STABILIZED!
COULD REALLY USE A DISTRACTION HERE!
IT'S OUT OF CONTROL!

I CAN SEE THE PALACE. IF I CAN GET THERE, I CAN GET TO BILLY!
TRY TO STAY TIGHT ON THE BLACK DRAGON! AT HIS SIZE, HE CAN'T MANEUVER IN CLOSE!
GOOD CALL. ALL RIGHT...HERE WE GO...
NICE TRY.
GHNN!
BUT YOU'RE NOT GETTING OFF THIS MOON, TOMMY.
WHO SAID ANYTHING...

...ABOUT LEAVING?
I COULD GET USED TO THIS LOW-GRAVITY THING.
YOU KNOW... IT SAYS AN AWFUL LOT...THAT YOU'LL ONLY FIGHT ME... WHEN YOU'RE THIRTY STORIES... TALL...
...
YOU'RE RIGHT.
I'D HATE TO GIVE ANY EXCUSES FOR LOSING.
AH, SEE...

...NOW YOU JUST MADE A BIG MIS--
HNN!
WHAM
WHAM
GHH!
NNNG!
WHAM
GOODBYE, TOMMY.
WHAT ARE YOU... WAITING FOR...
GAHH!

SCRAWNK
YOU'RE OKAY, MAN! I'VE GOT YOU! I'M TELEPORTING YOU BACK INSIDE--
UHHNNNN...

--NOW!
NNNG WHAT...ABOUT BILLY...
THE PUTTIES ARE FORTIFYING THE BASE, AND THE BLACK DRAGON'S COMING BACK. WE MISSED OUR SHOT.
WE GOTTA FIGURE OUT ANOTHER WAY.
"WAIT, SO HE'S STILL OUT THERE?"

I...THINK SO, YEAH. THE SIGNAL'S COMING FROM ALPHA, THAT'S FOR SURE.
OKAY, BUT IF HE'S SENDING US A SIGNAL, THAT MEANS HIS BACKUP SYSTEM'S GOTTA BE RUNNING, RIGHT? DOES THAT MEAN WE CAN SEND HIM A SIGNAL?
TRYING TO FIGURE THAT OUT... NOW...
R-RANGERS?
ALPHA!
TRINI! OH, HOW GOOD IT IS TO HEAR YOUR VOICE!
ARE YOU OKAY, ALPHA?!
I-I DON'T KNOW. MY OPERATING SYSTEMS ARE STILL FUNCTIONAL, BUT MOBILITY IS GONE. I'M IN PIECES, RANGERS!
WHERE ARE YOU?
AYE YI-YI...
...IN THE TRASH!
RITA SENT MY BODY TO BE MELTED DOWN FOR PARTS!
BUT NOT BEFORE I GOT A LOOK AT WHAT SHE'S DOING.
WHAT DO YOU--
GUYS!

I NEED A HAND!
WHOA! IS HE OKAY?!
TOMMY! WHAT HAPPENED?!
FINE... JUST NEED... A MINUTE...
THE BLACK DRAGON GOT US SEPARATED. TOMMY HELD HIS OWN FOR AS LONG AS HE COULD.
WHAT ABOUT BILLY?
WE COULDN'T GET TO HIM.
IS THIS... THE BLACK DRAGON'S?!
WE DON'T KNOW WHO OR WHAT THIS THING IS--FIGURED WE MIGHT BE ABLE TO, I DON'T KNOW, RUN A SCAN OR SOMETHING...?
JASON? IS THAT YOU?
ALPHA! ALPHA'S BACK?!
IT'S NICE TO HAVE SOME GOOD NEWS, RIGHT?

AS I WAS TELLING TRINI, MY BACKUP SYSTEMS ARE STILL FUNCTIONAL. BUT WITHOUT MY MAIN POWER SOURCE, I DON'T KNOW FOR HOW LONG.
ALPHA, YOU SAID YOU GOT A LOOK AT WHAT RITA'S DOING. WHAT DID YOU SEE?
WELL, YOUR POWERS AND ZORDS ARE BEING CONTROLLED BY THE BLACK DRAGON, WHO HAS ACCESS TO THE MORPHIN GRID THROUGH BILLY'S POWER COIN.
MY SPECTRAL SENSORS WATCHED HIS PHASE BLAST FILTER ONTO BILLY'S COIN.
BUT HOW? I MEAN, WHAT MAKES HIM ABLE TO ACTUALLY WARP OUR POWERS LIKE THIS? WHO IS THIS GUY?
I-I DON'T KNOW, KIMBERLY...
RITA'S DEADLINE IS ALMOST UP. WHICH MEANS THE ZORDS START ATTACKING CITIES.
WE'VE GOT TO FIGURE OUT A WAY TO GET OUR POWERS BACK.
CONTROL
BEFORE WE RUN OUT OF TIME.
"YOU HAD HIM IN YOUR GRASP--"

--AND YOU LET HIM GET AWAY. YOU LET THEM BOTH GET AWAY!
I... UNDERESTIMATED THE GREEN RANGER. IT WILL NOT HAPPEN AGAIN.
FRANKLY, I DON'T UNDERSTAND WHY YOU CAN'T JUST WARP HIS POWERS AWAY LIKE YOU'RE DOING TO THE OTHERS.
THE DRAGON COIN ACCESSES THE MORPHIN GRID IN A DIFFERENT WAY. AND BESIDES...WHEN I DESTROY THE GREEN RANGER, I WANT HIM TO BE AT FULL STRENGTH.
AND WHY IS THAT AGAIN?
YOU KNOW, WE SAW WHAT HAPPENED ON THE MOON. IF I DIDN'T KNOW ANY BETTER... I'D SAY IT ALMOST LOOKED LIKE YOU HESITATED.

I'M DOING ALL THIS FOR YOU, EMPRESS, BECAUSE YOU HAVEN'T BEEN ABLE TO CONQUER EARTH BY YOURSELF.
AND IT'S ALL JUST OUT OF THE GOODNESS OF YOUR HEART, IS IT?
ANNND YOUR NEW ARM IS ALL DONE!
MY MOTIVES ARE NONE OF YOUR CONCERN. THE ONLY THING I ASK IS THAT *I* BE THE ONE TO DESTROY THE GREEN RANGER.
SNAP
WHEN I ENCOUNTER HIM AGAIN, I WILL *NOT* HESITATE TO DELIVER THE FINAL BLOW.

SO ARE WE NOT GOING TO, UH, SPEAK AT ALL?
THERE IS NOTHING TO DISCUSS.
WELL, WE'RE, UH, BOTH PRISONERS. SO, WE HAVE THAT IN COMMON.
YOU ARE THE SWORN ENEMY OF MY EMPRESS AND I AM HER SWORN HONOR GUARD. WE HAVE NOTHING IN COMMON, BLUE RANGER.
...
IT'S JUST THAT, WELL, I DON'T KNOW EXACTLY HOW THINGS WORK WHERE YOU'RE FROM, BUT HERE...UH, ENEMIES OF ENEMIES ARE FRIENDS. AND, YOU KNOW, YOU'RE CHAINED TO THE FLOOR.
I GUESS I'M JUST WONDERING IF SHE STILL THINKS OF YOU THE SAME WAY YOU THINK OF HER...
...
MY EMPRESS KNOWS THE VALUE I PROVIDE. IN TIME, SHE WILL REMEMBER.
SHE HAS TO.

HEY.
HEY.

JASON SAID YOU WENT TOE-TO-TOE WITH THE DRAGON. THE THIRTY-STORIES-TALL VERSION.
I *TRIED* TO.
THAT'S PRETTY RIDICULOUS, MAN.
...YEAH. IN HINDSIGHT, *MAYBE* NOT ONE OF MY BEST IDEAS...

I OWE YOU AN APOLOGY.
JUST BECAUSE RITA PICKED YOU DOESN'T MEAN THERE'S SOMETHING BAD ABOUT YOU OR ANYTHING LIKE THAT.
YOU'RE GOING TO MAKE A REALLY GOOD RANGER.
AND...I'M SORRY I HAVEN'T DONE A BETTER JOB OF BACKING YOU.
I... APPRECIATE THAT, ZACK.
YEAH. I MEAN, LOOK, ONLY ONE OF US HERE HAS TAKEN ON A THIRTY STORY MONSTER BY THEMSELVES. EVEN IF IT MAYBE WASN'T THE BEST IDEA.
HEY, TRUST ME. AT THIS POINT, IF THERE WERE A WAY TO SWAP PLACES SO YOU COULD FIGHT HIM, I'D DO IT IN--

SO THE ARM IS MECHANICAL. SEE, I THOUGHT IT MIGHT BE. BUT IS THE REST OF HIM?
I DON'T KNOW. AND, TO SAY THIS IS "METAL"...IT'S NOT LIKE ANY METAL I'VE EVER SEEN.
HEY, THE PHASE BLAST TRICK THAT THE BLACK DRAGON USED ON US. CAN HIS ARM MAKE THAT KIND OF ENERGY?
I DON'T KNOW. I THINK SO? WHY?
WELL, YOU GUYS STILL HAVE YOUR POWERS. IT'S JUST...YOU'RE CUT OFF FROM THE MORPHIN GRID. RIGHT?
RIGHT...
SO THE ANSWER'S SIMPLE. YOU GUYS SHOULD JUST USE MINE.
WHAT DOES THAT MEAN?
THE PHASE BLAST BLACK DRAGON USED ON US IS THE SAME ONE ALPHA SAW HIM USE ON BILLY'S COIN. IT HAS TO BE. SO, WE DO THE SAME THING...BUT FILTER YOUR GUYS' MORPHING, THROUGH MINE.
WOULD THAT...EVEN WORK?
YES! SPLITTING THE GREEN RANGER POWERS AMONGST THE OTHERS WOULD PROVIDE AN ALTERNATE WAY TO ACCESS THE MORPHIN GRID.
BUT...IT WOULD LEAVE TOMMY POWERLESS!
TOMMY... ARE YOU SURE ABOUT THIS?
ME, BY MYSELF... I CAN'T STOP THIS. BUT YOU GUYS, TOGETHER...YOU CAN TAKE BACK YOUR ZORDS.
BESIDES, WHAT GOOD IS ONE POWER RANGER...
...WITHOUT THE OTHERS?

HEY, IT'S AT *LEAST* WORTH A SHOT, RIGHT?
MORE THAN A SHOT. EITHER WAY, THIS IS BIG OF YOU, MAN. I WANT YOU TO KNOW THAT.
THANKS.
LET'S DO IT.
ALL RIGHT, GUYS. IT'S MORPHIN TIME!
TYRANNOSAURUS!
PTERODACTYL!
SABERTOOTH TIGER!
MASTODON!
WHOA...

...THAT'S DIFFERENT...
TO BE CONTINUED...

THE ONGOING ADVENTURES OF
BULK & SKULL

WRITTEN BY
STEVE ORLANDO

ILLUSTRATED BY
CORIN HOWELL

COLORS BY
JEREMY LAWSON

LETTERS BY
JIM CAMPBELL

ANGEL GROVE YOUTH COURT.
FARKAS BULKMEIER! EUGENE SKULLOVITCH!
MY BROTHER, PRINCIPAL CAPLAN, WARNED ME ABOUT YOU. CONSTANTLY! NOW I FINALLY SEE WHY.
JUDGE

THE INFAMOUS BULK AND SKULL.

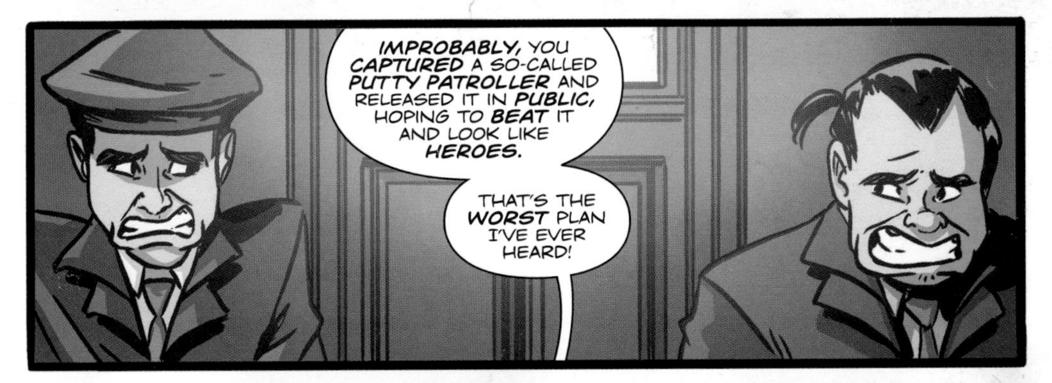
IMPROBABLY, YOU CAPTURED A SO-CALLED PUTTY PATROLLER AND RELEASED IT IN PUBLIC, HOPING TO BEAT IT AND LOOK LIKE HEROES.
THAT'S THE WORST PLAN I'VE EVER HEARD!

BUT IT GIVES ME AN IDEA. YOU WANTED TO BE HEROES? HERE'S YOUR CHANCE...
I SENTENCE YOU TO 1,993 HOURS OF COMMUNITY SERVICE, OVERSEEN BY A TRUE COMMUNITY SERVANT...

LIEUTENANT JEROME STONE!
OH NO. NOT HIM. THIS IS TERRIBLE. ANYONE BUT STONE.
YEAH, BULK! ANYONE WHO IS NOT STONE!
LOOK AT HIS POSTURE! LOOK AT HIS HAT! HE'S SO...HONEST. HE'S SO...LAME! HE'S SO...INTERESTED IN GRAMMARIZING!
YEAH, BULK! EVEN WORSE, HE'S...
RIGHT BEHIND US.
IT'S JUST "GRAMMAR," BULK. ONCE WE START ADDING SUFFIXES WHEREVER WE LIKE, CHAOS REIGNS.
GOOD GRAMMAR'S NO JOKE. READY TO HAVE SOME FUN?

ARTHUR NORVELL PUBLIC PARK. ANGEL GROVE.
KEEP PAINTING, BOYS. YOU'RE **REALLY** MAKING PROGRESS.
THIS IS A **DISASTER,** SKULL. THERE'S MORE PAINT ON **US** THAN THIS PLAYGROUND.
YEAH, BULK! THERE'S A **LOT** OF **PAINT!**
I **KNEW** WE SHOULDN'T HAVE SKIPPED ART CLASS.
IT'S SO **HOT,** SKULL. I'D SELL YOUR SOUL FOR AN **ICE CREAM.**
YEAH, BU-- WAIT, I WANTED AN ICE CREAM TOO!
RED
SORRY TO INTERRUPT, GENTLEMEN...

BREAK'S OVER.
...GRUMBLE YES, LIEUTENANT STONE GRUMBLE GRUMBLE...
THIS HAS TO STOP, SKULL. WE'LL NEVER FINISH. IT'S CRUEL AND UNUSUAL PUNISHMENT.
WORSE, BULK! IT'S MANDATORY!
JUST LOOK AT STONE. IT'S SEVEN HUNDRED DEGREES OUT AND HE'S DRINKING HOT COFFEE.
IT'S GOOD FOR THE CONSTITUTION. KEEPS THE BLOOD FLOWING, BOYS!
SEE THAT?! HOW DID HE EVEN HEAR US? STONE ISN'T HUMAN!
WAIT, THAT'S IT! IF WE CAN'T BEAT STONE, WE DO THE NEXT BEST THING! WE USE HIS POWERS FOR OUR BENEFIT.
WE HAVE TO BRING HIM OVER TO OUR SIDE.
BULK
SKULL
COP
OUR NEW AWESOME PLAN
OUR SIDE? HE'S RIGHT OVER THERE.
THAT'S RIGHT, SKULL. WE HAVE TO MAKE STONE PART OF THE GANG!

FRIDAY.
BE HONEST, STONE! BEING A POLICE OFFICER ISN'T EVEN A LITTLE BORING? THERE'S NOTHING YOU'D RATHER BE DOING? HAVING FUN, MAYBE?
JUSTICE IS A NONSTOP PARTY, GENTLEMEN.
SATURDAY.
IMAGINE TURNING THIS POOL INTO LEMONADE!
POOL RULES
SUGARY DRINKS HURT MY TEETH.
SUNDAY.
WHAT IF WE CUT OUR NAMES INTO THE LAWN?
AMBER'S SAND? SHOWS WHAT YOU KNOW, STONE, NO ONE OWNS A BEACH AROUND HERE.
DON'T BE RIDICULOUS. THIS MACHINE ISN'T EQUIPPED FOR AMPERSANDS.
IF YOU GUYS SPENT AS MUCH TIME WORKING AS YOU DID SCHEMING, YOU'D BE DONE WITH YOUR COMMUNITY SERVICE BY NOW.
STILL, I THINK YOU'VE EARNED A LUNCH BREAK.

MINUTES LATER.
CHES
I LOVE THIS PLACE!
YEAH, BULK! WE'VE BEEN FAMOUS HERE SINCE WE CALLED IN PRINCIPAL CAPLAN'S ORDER. THEY EVEN GAVE US OUR OWN SANDWICH!
ORD HER
HEADS UP PEOPLE, SANDWICH CELEBRITIES COMING THROUGH HERE.
GOOD AFTERNOON, MA'AM. WE'VE COME ON THIS FINE DAY, PLAGUED BY HUNGER AFTER HOURS OF HARD LABOR, TO ORDER A SANDWICH SO BOLD, SO FLAVORFUL...THAT IT COULD ONLY BE KNOWN BY ONE NAME...
THAT ICONIC BIT OF SANDWICH SORCERY KNOWN AS...
..."THE BULK."
I'M SORRY, SIR. WE DON'T CARRY "THE BULK" ANYMORE.
YOU...DON'T... CARRY..."THE BULK?"
IT'S UNBELIEVABLE. IT'S INCONCEIVABLE. SKULL!
THIS WILL NOT STAND!

ALL THIS OVER A SANDWICH, BULK?
YOU HAVE TO UNDERSTAND!
IT'S NOT JUST A SANDWICH! IT'S A SANDWICH WITH MY NAME ON IT! THEY LOVE ME AT SOKOLOSKI'S. THEY'RE ALWAYS SAYING "YOU AGAIN" WHEN I WALK IN.
I'VE GOT A PLAQUE NEXT TO THE PAPER TOWEL DISPENSER! THEY CAN'T DISCONTINUE "THE BULK."
HAVEN'T YOU EVER CARED ABOUT SOMETHING? HAVEN'T YOU EVER HAD A DREAM, ONLY TO HAVE THAT DREAM CRUMPLED UP IN A NAPKIN AND THROWN AWAY?
YOU HAVE TO LET US DO SOMETHING! YOU HAVE TO! IMAGINE IT WASN'T A SANDWICH...
Nooooooo
MOOORE
Coffee?
...IMAGINE IT WAS COFFEE!
COULD YOU JUST STAND BY AND DO NOTHING?

SOON AFTER.
"THE BULK'S THE BEST TO EAT! BEST ECONOMY FOR MEAT!"
YEAH!
GIMME THE MONEY!
SOMEBODY STOP HIM!
ON YOUR LEFT!
HEY! YOU! WERE YOU INSIDE? DID THEY PUT "THE BULK" BACK ON THE MENU?! DID THEY?
CAN THEY HEAR US OUT HERE? THEY NAMED A SANDWICH AFTER ME AND TOOK IT OFF THE MENU! THINK OF THE INJUSTICE! THINK OF IT!
JOIN US! JOIN US IN PROTEST!
DUDE, CHILL! YOU'RE FREAKING ME OUT! I'M--
--OUT OF--
TOSS
--HERE--
OOF!
SMACK!
I CAN'T BELIEVE IT, BUT SOMEHOW, I COULDN'T HAVE DONE THIS WITHOUT YOU. YOUR SANDWICH PASSION FOILED A ROBBERY! I'D SAY YOUR COMMUNITY SERVICE IS COMPLETE.
...DON'T ACT SURPRISED, STONE! YOU THINK I'D GET THAT ANGRY OVER A LITTLE OLD SANDWICH?
THIS WAS MY REAL PLAN. AFTER ALL...BULK AND SKULL ARE HEROES!
Next: BULK AND SKULL ARE NOT HEROES

COVER GALLERY

DAVID RYAN ROBINSON ▸ ISSUES FIVE–EIGHT ACTION FIGURE VARIANT COVERS

GREG SMALLWOOD ISSUE FIVE VILLAIN VARIANT COVER

RILEY ROSSMO | ISSUE FIVE VARIANT COVER

B.DEWEY
2016

KHARY RANDOLPH WITH COLORS BY **JOHN RAUCH** | ISSUE SEVEN VARIANT COVER

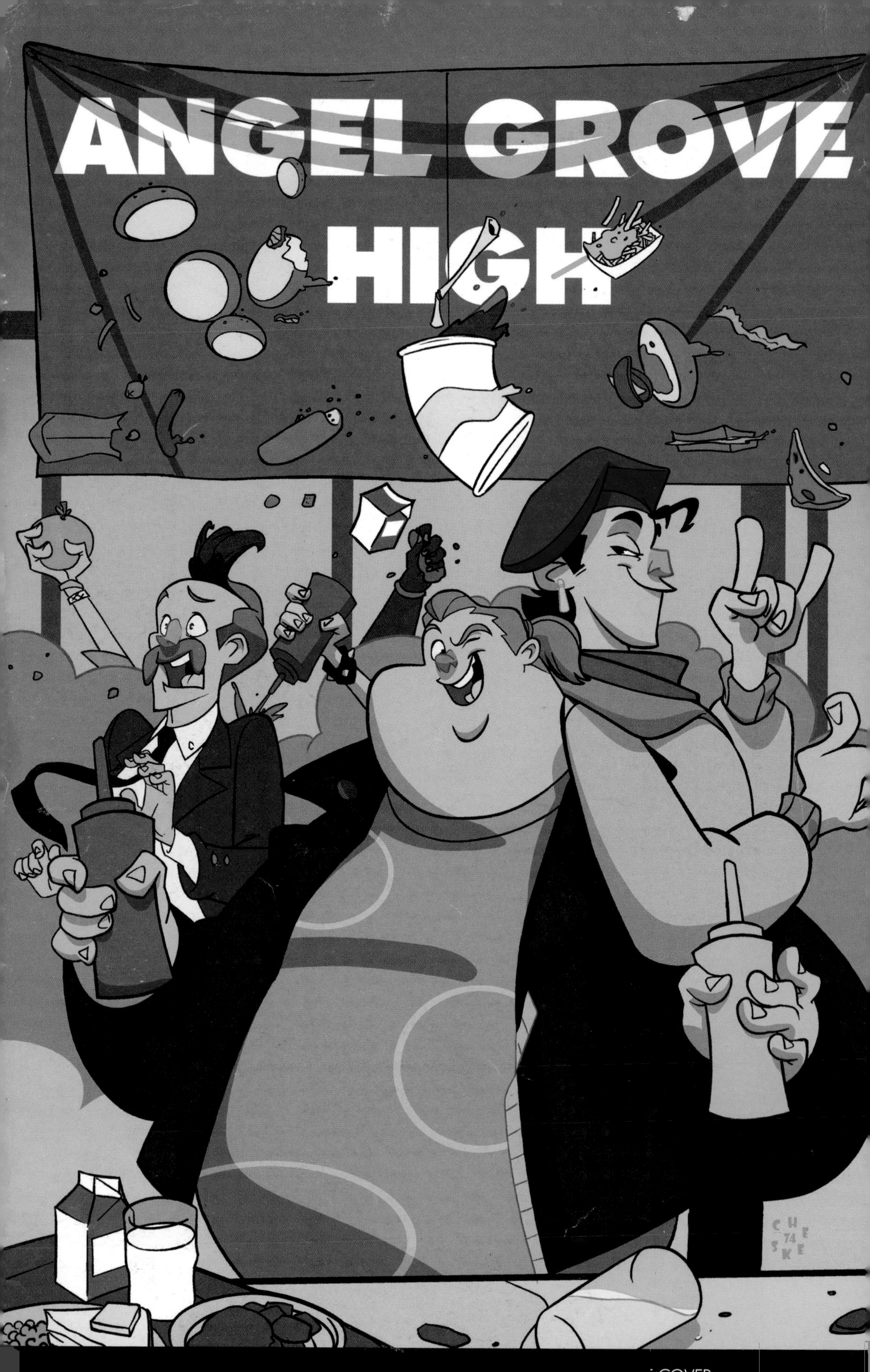
ANGEL GROVE
HIGH

VOLUME THREE

COMING IN 2017